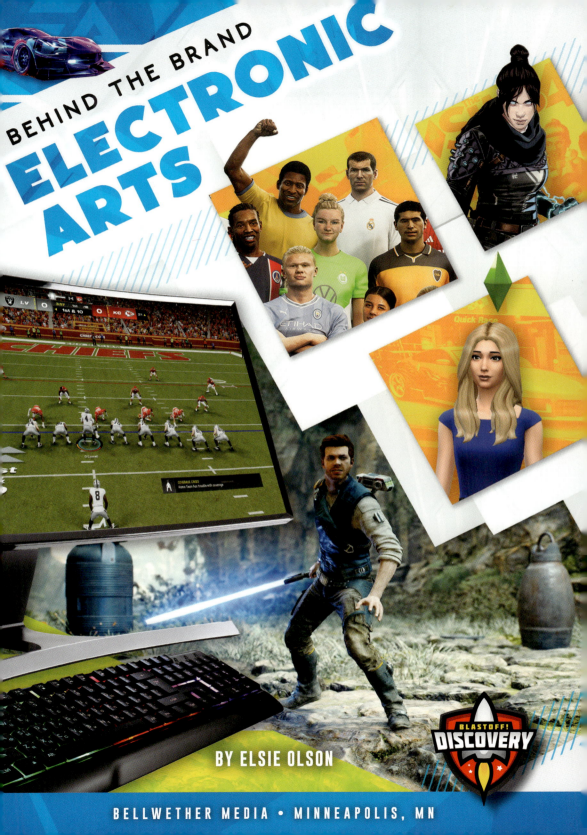

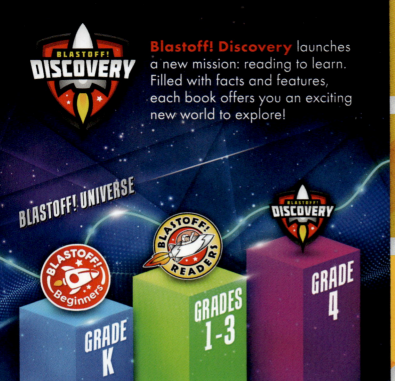

This is not an official Electronic Arts book. It is not approved by or connected with Electronic Arts, Inc.

This edition first published in 2025 by Bellwether Media, Inc.

No part of this publication may be reproduced in whole or in part without written permission of the publisher.
For information regarding permission, write to Bellwether Media, Inc.,
Attention: Permissions Department,
6012 Blue Circle Drive, Minnetonka, MN 55343.

Library of Congress Cataloging-in-Publication Data

LC record for Electronic Arts available at: https://lccn.loc.gov/2024021916

Text copyright © 2025 by Bellwether Media, Inc. BLASTOFF! DISCOVERY and associated logos are trademarks and/or registered trademarks of Bellwether Media, Inc. Bellwether Media is a division of Chrysalis Education Group.

Editor: Betsy Rathburn   Series Designer: Andrea Schneider   Book Designer: Josh Brink

Printed in the United States of America, North Mankato, MN.

TABLE OF CONTENTS

SATURDAY MORNING FOOTBALL	4
ELECTRONICS AND ART	6
GROWTH AND CHANGE	16
STAYING CONNECTED	26
PLAYING TOGETHER	28
GLOSSARY	30
TO LEARN MORE	31
INDEX	32

SATURDAY MORNING FOOTBALL

It is a rainy Saturday morning. It is too wet to play outside. Instead, a boy decides to hop on his Xbox. He logs into his EA Play account. He can access dozens of games from his favorite game company, Electronic Arts. But the boy knows just what game he wants to play.

Soon, he is running and passing as a player on the Oakland Raiders. The boy spends the rest of the morning playing *Madden NFL 24*. This is one of many fun EA games!

XBOX SERIES S

MADDEN NFL 24

ELECTRONICS AND ART

ELECTRONIC ARTS HEADQUARTERS
REDWOOD CITY, CALIFORNIA

Electronic Arts, or EA, is a video game company with **headquarters** in Redwood City, California. For more than 40 years, EA has produced some of the world's most popular video games.

Today, the company is split into two **divisions**. EA Sports oversees the company's sports-related **franchises**, including the Madden NFL, F1, and EA Sports FC series. EA Entertainment works on games such as the Star Wars and the Sims series. Fans all over the world enjoy playing EA games on computers and **consoles**!

ELECTRONIC ARTS HEADQUARTERS

REDWOOD CITY, CALIFORNIA

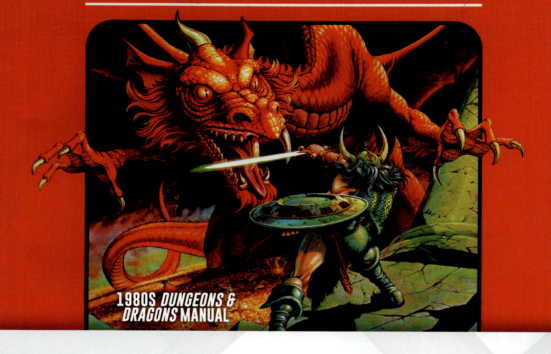

1980S *DUNGEONS & DRAGONS* MANUAL

Electronic Arts was founded by Trip Hawkins. Early in life, Trip loved playing games like *Strat-O-Matic Football*. Later, he liked to play *Dungeons & Dragons*. He enjoyed how these games challenged his mind while also building connections with others.

FOOTBALL FUN

Before he started EA, Trip made his own football-themed board game. Players loved the game, but it did not sell well. Still, it taught Trip a lot about running his own business.

During the 1970s, computers were changing quickly. Trip believed personal computers were the future of gaming. He planned to start a computer game business. But he needed to wait for the technology to improve. By the time Trip graduated from Stanford University in 1978, he was ready for a job in the computer **industry**.

STANFORD UNIVERSITY

APPLE II PERSONAL COMPUTER

In 1978, Trip got a job at Apple. The year before, the company had released the Apple II personal computer. Trip was excited to help Apple **market** its personal computers. He learned about business and watched for the right time to start his game company.

10

That moment came in 1982. Trip quit his job at Apple and started Amazin' Software. Early employees did not like the name. They felt it did not reflect the company's **mission**. Amazin' Software changed its name to Electronic Arts. Now it was time to make some games.

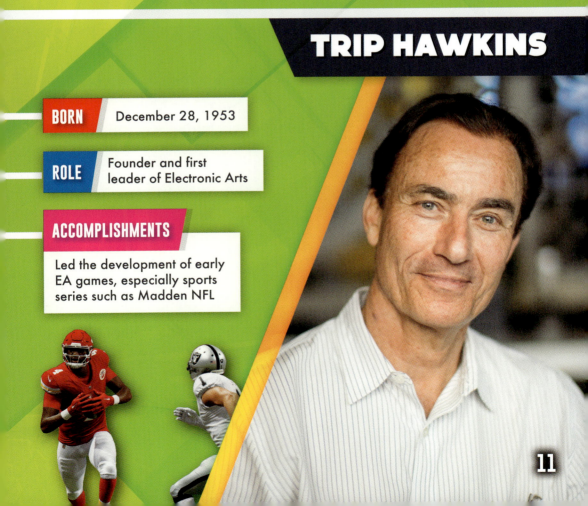

TRIP HAWKINS

BORN December 28, 1953

ROLE Founder and first leader of Electronic Arts

ACCOMPLISHMENTS

Led the development of early EA games, especially sports series such as Madden NFL

11

On May 20, 1983, EA shipped out its first batch of games. Its first-ever game was *Hard Hat Mack*, a **platform game** about a construction worker. *M.U.L.E.* was another early game. This **strategy game** was one of the first important multiplayer games.

THE BERRY BEST

Danielle Bunten Berry was the lead designer on *M.U.L.E.* In 2009, she was named one of the top 100 game designers of all time.

HARD HAT MACK

EARLY EA GAME PACKAGING

Early EA games got good reviews. The company stood out because of its sales and marketing. Games were packaged to look like music albums. Magazine **advertisements** highlighted game designers as if they were rock stars. Instead of using **distributors** like most game companies, EA sold games directly to stores.

During this time, the video game industry was changing. There were too many consoles on the market. Games were low quality. Sales fell, and many console companies went out of business. EA decided to focus more on high-quality computer games than console games.

One of the company's biggest early computer games was *One on One: Dr. J vs. Larry Bird*. Players loved this basketball game. It sold more than 1 million copies for the Apple II. The game proved EA was a serious competitor in the game industry. It also showed that sports games could be top sellers.

ADVERTISEMENT FOR *ONE ON ONE: DR. J VS. LARRY BIRD*

ELECTRONIC ARTS TIMELINE

1982
Trip Hawkins starts the company that will become Electronic Arts

1987
EA releases its first games developed in-house

1983
EA ships its first batch of games

1988
The Madden NFL series starts with the release of *John Madden Football*

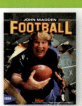

1994
Trip leaves EA

2000
EA releases *The Sims*, the first game in the Sims franchise

2013
EA gets the rights to make Star Wars games

2014
EA launches EA Access

2023
EA divides into two divisions, EA Sports and EA Entertainment

ALL-STAR ACTION

One on One: Dr. J vs. Larry Bird featured real-life basketball stars Julius Erving and Larry Bird. It was the first game that let gamers play as real athletes!

15

GROWTH AND CHANGE

EA GAME DESIGNERS

For its first five years, EA had only released games created by outside game designers. But it wanted to create more games itself. Making good games took time. EA hired programmers and artists to work on games. This gave the company more control over the games it released.

In 1987, EA released *Skate or Die!* for the Commodore 64 computer. This was the company's first in-house game. Players chose from four characters to compete in different skateboarding events. They raced downhill, did tricks, and more! Many more games that were created in-house followed.

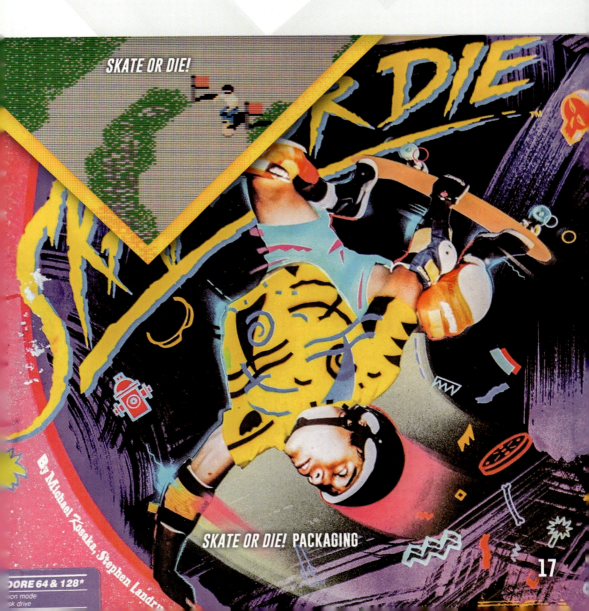

SKATE OR DIE!

SKATE OR DIE! PACKAGING

17

EA was gaining success. But Trip wanted to do more. He had always dreamt of making a football game. In 1984, he met with football coach John Madden. Trip told Madden his idea for a video game with 7 players on each team. But Madden thought the teams should have 11 players, just like a real football game.

EARLY EA SPORTS GAMES

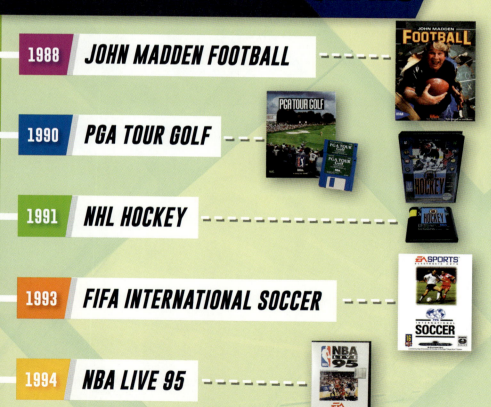

1988	JOHN MADDEN FOOTBALL
1990	PGA TOUR GOLF
1991	NHL HOCKEY
1993	FIFA INTERNATIONAL SOCCER
1994	NBA LIVE 95

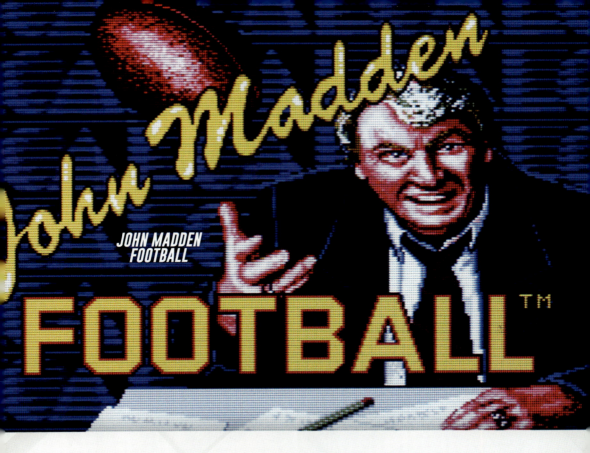

This made the game much more complicated. At the time, personal computers were not powerful enough to easily run such a game. But after years of work, *John Madden Football* was released in 1988. The game mirrored real football. Players could run different plays. It was a hit!

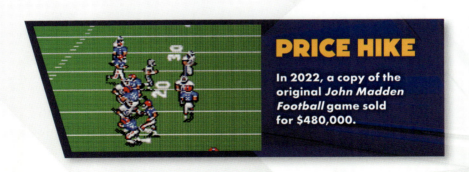

PRICE HIKE

In 2022, a copy of the original *John Madden Football* game sold for $480,000.

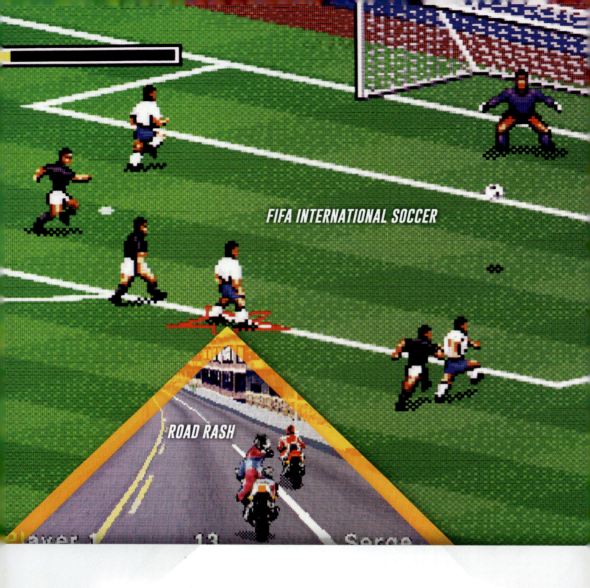

FIFA INTERNATIONAL SOCCER

ROAD RASH

In time, EA began releasing more games for consoles. By the early 1990s, it made games for Sega and Nintendo as well as for computers. The 1993 game *FIFA International Soccer* was a big seller on the Sega Genesis. Players loved its realistic look and sound effects. Many more FIFA games followed. Other popular series that started during this time were NHL Hockey and Road Rash.

In 1994, Trip left the company. But EA continued to grow. It added new games and grew its many franchises. Series such as The Need for Speed and PGA Tour Golf sold well.

A NEW DIRECTION

In 2022, EA's partnership with FIFA ended. This meant no more FIFA games. But EA soon replaced this series with the EA Sports FC soccer series!

PGA TOUR GOLF

THE NEED FOR SPEED

MAXIS COFOUNDER WILL WRIGHT

THE SIMS

The company began buying game **studios** in the 1990s. In 1997, EA bought Maxis. In 2000, EA and Maxis released *The Sims*. Players could build houses, get jobs, and meet neighbors. Many **sequels** and **expansion packs** followed. The franchise has since sold more than 200 million copies!

SNOWBOARD SUCCESS

SSX was released in 2000. This snowboarding game let players do wild tricks as they raced down hills. More games followed. The series has sold millions of copies!

In the late 1990s and early 2000s, EA got the **rights** to make games based on James Bond movies. *Tomorrow Never Dies* came out in 1999. Players fought and spied as James Bond. Several more Bond games followed.

SIMS EXPANSION PACKS

THE SIMS: MAKIN' MAGIC

Released: 2003
New Feature: Sims can use magic

THE SIMS 2: PETS

Released: 2006
New Feature: Sims can own pets, and players can design their own pet

THE SIMS 3: ISLAND PARADISE

Released: 2013
New Feature: Sims live on an island and can scuba dive, set up resorts, and live on houseboats

THE SIMS 4: SNOWY ESCAPE

Released: 2020
New Feature: Sims can snowboard, ski, and climb mountains

In 2013, EA got the rights to make Star Wars games. The company began making games for the Star Wars: Battlefront series in 2015 with *Star Wars Battlefront*. Players explored planets and battled enemies. Many other Star Wars games followed, including 2023's *Star Wars Jedi: Survivor*.

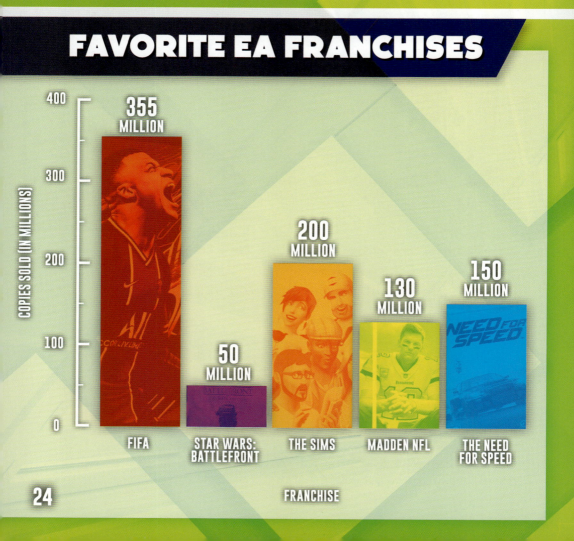

Apex Legends

Apex Legends came out in 2019. By 2021, this **battle royale** game had over 100 million players! In 2024, *Tales of Kenzera: ZAU* was released. This game lets players fight enemies and unlock new paths. EA always has fun new games to discover!

ONLINE EXCITEMENT

In the 2010s, online gaming grew. In 2014, EA launched EA Access. Its name was later changed to EA Play. The service lets players pay for access to a library of many EA games!

STAYING CONNECTED

2022 EA EDUCATION PROGRAM

EA works to make the world a better place. In 2017, EA launched a digital learning program called Play to Learn. This program teaches students educational topics in a fun way. It helps them learn about different careers. In 2023, the program reached 15,500 students.

HELPING HANDS

EA encourages employees to give back. It matches money that employees give to help support different organizations.

In 2023, the company gave $1 million to support science, math, and art education. EA also gives millions of dollars to the EA Madden **Scholarship** Program. Each year, the program provides 24 students with scholarships to attend historically Black colleges and universities.

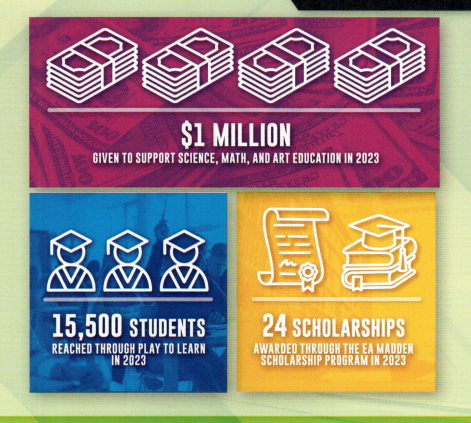

GIVING BACK

$1 MILLION
GIVEN TO SUPPORT SCIENCE, MATH, AND ART EDUCATION IN 2023

15,500 STUDENTS
REACHED THROUGH PLAY TO LEARN IN 2023

24 SCHOLARSHIPS
AWARDED THROUGH THE EA MADDEN SCHOLARSHIP PROGRAM IN 2023

PLAYING TOGETHER

EA fans connect with others through their favorite games. Gamers can play together online. EA also hosts **esports** competitions for some of its most popular games. These include the Madden NFL and EA Sports FC series, as well as *Apex Legends*. The Madden Championship Series is a popular competition. The top Madden players compete for prizes. In 2024, the Ultimate Madden Bowl had a $1 million prize pool!

EA is committed making high-quality games. With new games and favorite franchises, EA continues to push the limits of gaming!

ULTIMATE MADDEN BOWL

WHAT IT IS

A competition to decide the best Madden NFL player in the world

WHERE IT IS

2024 finals held in Las Vegas, Nevada

HOW TO WATCH

Fans can watch live over YouTube and Twitch

GLOSSARY

advertisements—public notices that tell people about products, services, or events

battle royale—related to a type of game in which many players compete to be the last player or team standing

consoles—electronic devices mainly used for playing video games

distributors—companies that sell products to stores

divisions—groups within companies

esports—related to video games played competitively

expansion packs—additional content that can be added to an existing game to add new items, characters, or other features

franchises—collections of books, movies, or other media that are related to one another

headquarters—a company's main office

industry—a group of businesses that provide a certain product

market—to advertise or promote something for sale

mission—an official goal or purpose

platform game—a game in which characters jump on platforms to get to new places

rights—a legal claim to something

scholarship—related to money given to help people attend school

sequels—games that continue the story started in a game that came before it

strategy game—a game in which players use decision-making skills to complete goals and beat the game

studios—places where games are made

TO LEARN MORE

AT THE LIBRARY

Bolte, Mari. *Super Surprising Trivia about Video Games*. North Mankato, Minn.: Capstone Press, 2024.

Mooney, Carla. *Electronic Arts: Makers of Madden NFL and The Sims*. Minneapolis, Minn.: Abdo Publishing, 2024.

Polinsky, Paige V. *Nintendo*. Minneapolis, Minn.: Bellwether Media, 2023.

ON THE WEB

FACTSURFER

Factsurfer.com gives you a safe, fun way to find more information.

1. Go to www.factsurfer.com.

2. Enter "Electronic Arts" into the search box and click 🔍.

3. Select your book cover to see a list of related content.

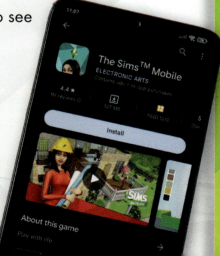

INDEX

advertisements, 13, 14
Apex Legends, 25, 28
Apple, 10, 11, 14
Berry, Danielle Bunten, 12
computers, 7, 9, 10, 14, 17, 19, 20
consoles, 5, 7, 14, 20
designers, 12, 13, 16
EA Entertainment, 7
EA Madden Scholarship Program, 27
EA Play, 5, 25
EA Sports, 7
EA Sports FC (franchise), 7, 21, 28
early EA sports games, 18
esports, 28
fans, 7, 28
favorite EA franchises, 24
FIFA (franchise), 20, 21
franchises, 7, 20, 21, 22, 23, 24, 28
games, 5, 8, 12, 14, 15, 17, 18, 19, 20, 21, 22, 23, 24, 25, 28

giving back, 27
Hawkins, Trip, 8, 9, 10, 11, 18, 21
John Madden Football, 18, 19
Madden, John, 18
Madden NFL (franchise), 5, 7, 18, 19, 28, 29
name, 11
One on One: Dr. J vs. Larry Bird, 14, 15
packaging, 13, 17
Play to Learn, 26
Redwood City, California, 6, 7
sales, 14, 22, 24
Sims expansion packs, 23
Sims, The (franchise), 7, 22, 23
Star Wars (franchise), 7, 24
studios, 22
timeline, 15
Ultimate Madden Bowl, 28, 29

The images in this book are reproduced through the courtesy of: Gabe Hilger, front cover (*Madden NFL 24*, *Star Wars Jedi: Survivor*), pp. 5 (*Madden NFL 24*), 11 (*Madden NFL 24*), 25 (bottom); Manuel Findeis, front cover (computer); Christina Leaf, front cover (Sims character), p. 2; Paul Stringer, front cover (The Need for Speed game); Diego Thomazini, front cover (FIFA game), pp. 21 (top), 24 (Madden NFL game); Miguel Lagoa, front cover (F1 game); Cassiano Correia, front cover (*Apex Legends*), p. 24 (FIFA game); bertys30/ Deposit Photos, front cover (Sims game); Instacodez, front cover (The Need for Speed car); Lukmanazis, pp. 3, 25 (*Apex Legends*); LSOphoto, pp. 4-5; Iryna Bauer, p. 5 (Xbox Series S); Pauras, p. 6; drserg, p. 7; David Pimborough/ Alamy, p. 8 (top); oasisamuel, p. 8 (football); achinthamb, p. 9; Ivan Arkhipov, p. 10; Christopher Michel/ Wikipedia, p. 11; Gracefool/ Wikipedia, p. 12 (*M.U.L.E.*); Happy Go Lucky Living/ eBay, p. 12 (*Hard Hat Mack*); Roger Ressmeyer/ Getty Images, p. 13; Electronic Arts/ Wikipedia, p. 14; Bonus/ Wikipedia, pp. 15 (1988 entry), 18 (*John Madden Football*); Mika1h, p. 15 (2000 entry); Pe3k, p. 15 (2013 entry), 24 (Star Wars: Battlefront game, The Need for Speed game); Focus On Sport/Getty Images, p. 15 (bottom); Christopher Morris - Corbis/ Getty Images, p. 16; ArcadeImages/ Alamy, pp. 17 (*Skate or Die!*), 19 (all), 20 (*FIFA International Soccer*), 21 (*PGA Tour Golf*, *The Need for Speed*), 22 (*The Sims*, *SSX*); jaysav-34/ ebay, p. 17 (*Skate or Die!* packaging); RagingKinezo Gaming, p. 18 (*PGA Tour Golf*); ELECTRONIC GAMING ONLINE, p. 18 (*NHL Hockey*); Techtri/ Wikipedia, p. 18 (*FIFA International Soccer*); BlackstarAssets, p. 18 (NBA Live 95); AFP/ Stringer/ Getty Images, p. 22; Sue Leaf, p. 23 (top left); Import Export Emporium/ ebay, p. 23 (top right); dealswithgio/ ebay, p. 23 (bottom left); jeanneth007/ ebay, p. 23 (bottom right); Jimmy Tudeschi, p. 24 (Sims game); ASSOCIATED PRESS/ AP Newsroom, p. 26; ricochet64, p. 26 (bottom); ElenaR, p. 27 (top); Drazen Zigic, p. 27 (bottom left); insta_photos, p. 27 (bottom right); Sean M. Haffey/ Getty Images, p. 28; Miikka Skaffari/ Getty Images, p. 29; Chase D'animulls, p. 31 (top); Maor_Winetrob, p. 31 (bottom).